Poems of
REISEN CAUL

REISEN CAUL

WESTBOW·
PRESS
A DIVISION OF THOMAS NELSON
& ZONDERVAN

WestBow Press books may be ordered through booksellers or by contacting:

WestBow Press
A Division of Thomas Nelson & Zondervan
1663 Liberty Drive
Bloomington, IN 47403
www.westbowpress.com
1 (866) 928-1240

ISBN: 978-1-4908-8085-3 (sc)

Library of Congress Control Number: 2015911029

Print information available on the last page.

WestBow Press rev. date: 07/10/2015

Dedicated To Jah

In memory of the woman with the alabaster box of precious ointment who poured the ointment on the head of Jesus doing it for His burial as He sat at meat.

Contents

Introduction

The simplicity of life is so easy that a child can
understand but the older one gets
the more one makes life so complicated.
Wisdom comes to the aged, and many
learn to go back to simplicity. Oh, if mankind
can only feel the hurt the **Heart** of
God carries for the souls He created to love Him, and yet, they don't.

To know the Maker is to receive His perfect
living sacrifice; (which is His Only Begotten Son who came out of His bosom). The
Maker of everything is Almighty
God, whose name is **"I AM"** who has seven
Spirits with nine attributes. **"I AM"** is
the Almighty Maker of Heaven and earth and
all there is; who always was, is and
always will be. His Only Begotten Son is His **Heart**.

Land Ho!

Camouflage your dreams, and never let one know...
It'll spoil your surprise, and take away your hope---
Set your eyes on waters that float through halls of time
Imagine you're a sailor in the vastness of your mind.
Press to your destiny, where you see only blue...
It's a primary color; it is your biggest clue---
Beckoning you to clouds, that hang up overhead;
Sunshine will fall down right upon your bed.
Where's it coming from? It's only God who knows...
Tears well up, and drip; falling down your nose---
Tiny bells will ring, and you will say, "Land Ho!"
You are at the helm, but God is pulling your boat.
Seas will pass away, and dreams will be fulfilled...
Rainy days will pass, and clouds float over hills---
Lilies in the valley will be your bed of joy;
Pastures green are mixtures of golden blues---"Ahoy!"

The Good Shepherd

A wandering Christian is a wandering Jew...
Wanting to know how to be a chosen few---
Living in pleasure is not what's to choose...
Donning the holy is what man must do---
How can man do that if he doesn't know how...
Living in the Word, and praying as he vows---
To do what God says---never straying on his own...
Following His lead as He takes His own home---
Forsaking the flesh, but only in His power...
How can one know, but to believe in each hour---
That God'll come through to always save the day---
Before the lamb dies to show him the way.

True Rebirth

Open my eyes, and open my ears---
Let me repent, and please dry my tears...
Soften my heart, and won't You come in
To free me from self, and all of my sin?
I humbly bow at the Almighty Throne;
I want regeneration through Jesus, Your Son---
Make me anew, and give me new life;
That I can only have through the Lord, Jesus Christ.
I put away all my self-righteousness---
I put away all of my own consciousness...
I never want sin in my life anymore;
I hear Your soft knocking at my heart's door.
Come in! Come in, and sit on the throne
Of my heart forever, and make it Your home---
And then, I'll be baptized in the washing of water
To receive Your Holy Spirit's ultimate power;
To live unto You, and make You my Lord...
I promise to always live in Your Word.
Keep me from straying; don't break my legs---
I want Your way only; this plea's what I beg.
Lead me along the straight, narrow path,
Hide me away from Your most dreaded wrath;
Let me bow hourly on my knees in prayer,
And let me always see Your tender care.
Everyday that I live let Your favor cover me...
I give You all glory, and it's all for Thee---
For I want nothing more than to be by Your side
Through the thick 'n the thin of this temporal life;
And when it is o'er I want to shine like a star...
So, teach me to know how to play out my part.
Overflow me with love, so others can come,
And together we all can raise hands to the Son!

My Earnest Prayer

Teach me to know how to live and grow
As a flower on the olive tree...
To bud it's fruit, and make it's oil;
To anoint Your head and feet.
Show me a picture You painted of me
That was in Your mind long ago...
Of what I would look like completed in You;
So, I can have something to hold.
Help me to see what You long for me to be
To help me press on to the mark
Of the *High Calling* You have for me
On the journey I started to embark.
Teach me to know all of Your ways,
And in You know how to stand---
Let my leaves crown Your head with glory,
And put peace and good will in Your hand.
Let the luxury of Your wealth, and oils
Soothe my daily walk...
Let more fruit bear to crown You with
As it continues to grow on the stalk.
Let majesty reign in my mortal being
So, my life will give You praise...
Let all the world see Love in me
So, they'll be drawn to faith.

Be Still

Be still, and know that I am *God*...
Rest in the Word *Alone*...
Kneel, and bow; Jehovah *Is Lord*...
And the King will be on His Throne.
Be patient, and wait until I *Call*...
Find peace through prayer in *My*
Eternal rest to your weary *Soul*;
And death will pass you by.
My burden is easy; My yoke is *Light*...
Walk step in step with *Me*...
Wash daily, and nightly in My *Word*,
And the Judge will set you free.
Fulfill the law, and live in *Love*...
And nothing shall offend *You*...
Put on your armour *Everyday*,
And the darts won't even prick you.
Until the end just keep the *Faith*...
And run the race that *Wins*...
Reach the lost; turn many to *Me*...
Let the Lamb's blood cover your sins.
Do not fear what man can *Do*...
Flesh just comes to *Naught*...
Keep My Commandments, and do not *Stray*...
For your soul's already been bought.
Put flesh away; let My Spirit *Lead*...
For I am right, and *Holy*...
I am Truth, and I am *Love*...
I made you to desire Me only.
Be ye perfect, for I am *Perfect*...
And grace will get you *By*...
The arm of flesh will fail *You*...
Without Me you can't fly.
Legalism is not what's *Right*...

No man can pluck you *Away*...
You're in My hand *Eternally*...
So, always let Me reign.
Die to self, and you're *Desires*...
Let My Son come shining *Through*...
Get out of the way; for I give *Life*...
And will lead you in all you do.
Do not stray, and you'll do *Well*...
My love for you is *Through*
My Son who gave His life for *You*...
In Me, you can be new.
I'll lead you by still waters *Amid*...
Green pastures surrounding *Streams*...
So, you won't thirst---just think *Of Peace*;
And live in happy dreams.

The Humble Road

Lilies are clothed with purity...
Birds are fed in obscurity---
Man toils and spins around,
And plunders to win a crown.
Reason with God to see
Your pardon for sins that be...
It's faith that pleases the Father,
And many make such a bother.
Everything from God's given freely...
Man's blinded, and cannot see---
He follows the Gentile's ways,
And God is left at bay.
It's sad that people are lost
In ways that have a cost---
Vanity paves their highway...
The humble road's the right way.
The highway sees all the construction...
Man's eyes see only obstruction---
The narrow path is all dusty;
It's a walk that makes one husky.
The narrow path holds many diamonds...
Deep in the ground they're shinin'---
What glitters, and sparkles on highways
Are broken glass in the freeways.

Oh, Death

Oh, death, how can I fear you? You have no sting---
I live among nature in solitude; with every good thing.
I dreamt of hell to see what it entails,
(And I dreamt of Heaven in contrast to the ails)
Knowing souls are blinded forever; taunting voices o'er
Where hope is slammed down eternally.
I dreamt also of being suspended in nothing but grey
Like grey matter that takes up most of the brain---
And there was no gravity.

At first, I was apprehensive wondering where I was---
Then, my Jesus showed up out of nowhere, because
He knew I needed comfort immediately, it seemed,
And a great peace came over me; I saw in my dream,
But He popped up on my right side, and then on my left;
Then, on my right---giving me preference previously.
I dreamt it was with only mental telepathy we spoke,
I verbalized as He looked at me with a *faraway look*---
His eyes were directing me.

In the distance I saw a circle that spun with flames---
Looking closer, I saw tiny, white souls jumping in pain.
Their tiny voices were screaming like ants,
But, they were pure white, and I recognized by chance
People I knew. I gaped. I pointed. He turned my head
To see a teardrop roll down His cheek.
"Don't cry, Jesus," I said. "They didn't want you at all!"
He turned His head back...that *faraway look* was tall---
"You still love them, don't You," I peeked.

The Path of Life

"Ism" is a religion----and people babble on
Schism is a division----and half the church is gone
Ashram is an exertion----and common to a lot
Chasm is an interruption----a breach without a plot

Papal is a staple----adjoining good and bad
Able was unable----and Cain; a wretched cad
Label is a table----depicting this from that
Fable is a tale----an allegoric chat

Daze is a craze----confusion to dazzle on
Maze is a phase----through a labyrinth to anon
Gaze at the gays----and nothing seems to happen
Plays are a stage----to trigger solemn laughin'

Faith is a gate----by grace to find a path
Eighth of the race----can say God has a wrath
Hafiz is a way----to a kingdom that's a bath
Hate is a plate----of misfortune many hath

Tishri is a firstly----that brought a noble offspring
Astarte is an "iffy"----a man created gagging
Trimurti is a bursting----a triune with destroying
Trinity is a thirsting----no circular eternal thing

Truth is but a one----and few can find the way
Ruth was a woman----who brought a King they say
Roots grow deep and strong----eyes see what may
Clues are all along----the path of Life to save.

What People Love

People love to glamorize evil institutions;
People love to meddle, and make such intrusions...
People love to always play God Almighty;
People love to worship those high, and mighty---

People love to pride themselves; taking God's glory
People love to exaggerate every little story...
People love to elevate intellectual rhetoric---
People love to say how great was Frederick.

People love mythology, and every little lie;
People love to keep fairy tales alive...
People love to always worship the dead---
People like to slither like snakes in a bed.

People like to idolize everything that's bad;
People love perversion, and call it, "So Rad!"
People love no conscience, and nothing that is good---
People love extremeness, and things in "the hood."

People love to tempt God, and infuriate Him, too...
People love violence, and nothing that's true---
People love torture, and hatred, and crime;
People love to steal from the innocent, and blind---

People love the devil who was kicked out of Heaven
People love money, and they love to eat leaven---
People love Darkness instead of the Light;
People love nothing that is called just, and right...

But His Hand is stretched out still---(Isaiah 5:25)

Freedom

Freedom comes at such a high price,
But it's not for freedom to sin...
It's freedom to live from tyranny,
And freedom to worship, but then,

What does one worship; whom does one love?
That is a matter of choice.
Freedom to do as anyone pleases
Is chaos with a booming voice.

Tyranny can happen in the United States---
There's nothing new under the sun.
All that's been done has been done before,
And what new lands can be won?

Earth is limited, and getting smaller
Through internet, and communication.
People flounder without any leaders
To guide them to the right direction.

All we like sheep have gone astray...
Each, and everyone---
Can the world come around to find new life
In Jesus Christ, the Son?

People imagine such vanity,
And money's the name of the game...
A faithless, and perverse generation we are,
But where can we put the blame?

Choice Is A Gift

If culture is demons, dragons, and idols,
I'd rather remain uncultured.
It seems a bit ridiculous, and vain
To be torn, and eaten by vultures.

If long ago thinking is classical art,
Because of an empire church
That extorted, and sought the blood of many;
Who controlled, and loved money to hurt---

It seems progression of thought should abate
The tragedies of life now dead---
Where kings, and rulers thirsted for power,
And suffered short life spans in bed.

It's tears that purify the soul,
But doesn't mean it's salvation...
Like water only gets one wet
Without internal regeneration.

There comes a time in everyone's life
Where truth just passes them by---
But those who seek it can hold on, and grab
It's treasures and learn how to fly.

Man has no wings like angels do,
And blinders can stop a thought---
To lead a person to a horrible end,
And bring his destiny to naught.

I imagine it's better to read what is true
Then imagine fallacies of the mind,
Because what can tragedy do for a soul
That continuously wants to be blind?

It's pride at its best that puffs up self
For many with low self-esteem,
Because they can't ever find the rest
They desperately try to achieve.

It only can come to childlike innocence---
Salvation through God's only Son;
Whose hearts are prepared by God alone,
Though, it's offered to everyone.

Man is a creature created to love,
But lust interposes its lies
To distract those who only want emptiness,
And love Death better than Life.

It's selfish, and vain to play a martyr role...
It's disturbing to let others choose
A person's final destination in life,
Because in the end they both lose.

One must be responsible to know;
Choice is an individual gift;
To let another take that away
Is a log in the water adrift.

Free Will

God made man to love Him---worship and adore
Everything about Him; God wants to give him more

Than nature's beauty fair---more than rain and sun,
More than earthly living; God wants him to be one

Forever in His goodness---eternal life in Him;
Beyond what man can know; places in perfection.

God's patience overwhelms us---if we open up;
God hurts inside His being; for man rejects His love...

Love is that which conquers---every vile thing;
Love is peace and safety; it goes against man's being.

Man rather chooses hatred---'tis easier to do;
Rebellion is as stubborn; as a pigheaded goatish mule

To have God's love so freely---choice is faith alone
Grace gives it power; to ask and bring it home.

If one's heart is opened---to everlasting Love...
Salvation is a present; that comes down from above.

Repentance from all evil---must be number one
Before receiving Jesus; God's only b'gotten Son.

Thankfulness is after---choosing the pure Word
To grow in all His splendor; covered in His power

To fight the evil forces---now, and not be torn;
Armour must be polished; ready to be worn.

It's choices that God gives---every living core;
Choose wisely on this earth; once dead, it is no more.

The Mystery of Mastery

Man chooses science, knowledge, wisdom, and math,
And opts to leave the source all behind---
He'd rather pick self-glorification;
He thinks he creates, but he's blind.
So, what blinds man to life's meaning and truth?
...the Creator who won't share His glory.
It's a pity to think so highly of one's self
'Cause it blocks out the only true story.
Life has a plot; it's not chaotic, nor haphazard...
Happiness is fleeting; it's opposite is sadness.
Love is not earthly, devilish, nor carnal
And truth is the real key to gladness.
Age can kill time if one lives to one's self,
And time can slow down with true love...
Agape and phileo are loves Heavenly giv'n---
While Eros is idolatrous love.

The Mortality of Mortals

What is the purpose to be educated
If ignorance is bliss?
Is it to gain to one's hurt in life,
And live in a world amiss?

Knowledge continuously increases,
But society continues to fail.
God chooses base things of this world
While rich and famous wail.

Is fun real fun, or is laughter the joke
That makes the world go 'round?
Through ages the powerful all die young,
So, why should one abound?

Everything's boring after awhile,
And everyone lives in prison.
Will peace truly ever be attained,
If there's always a constant schism?

If life is death, it'll cancel out,
And God is not unknowing
To all the calamities of man,
And all his sufferings and groanings.

For God to die in human form
To save the lost from hell...
Man must die to what he wants,
And surrender all of himself;

And freely repent, and ask for a Saviour
To dwell inside the soul
And wash away original sin,
So man can be made whole...

And cut away the flesh attached
To the spirit, and the body
For if a man dies in his sins,
He'll not be among the godly.

God will prosper, and keep His own,
Underneath His wing
Even though His children suffer,
Eternally they'll sing...

Some were born to never seek
Salvation from the Lord,
Because the world has opposites;
Free will's an open door.

Legalism is not grace;
We're saved by grace through faith.
If flesh tries to conquer sin,
It no longer can be grace;

Faith's the victory that overcomes,
And self must be behind
So, Jesus gets all the glory and
No man can cross that line.

There's Nothing New Under The Sun

The wisest man in the world once said,
"There's nothing new under the sun."
Every new thing man thinks is grand,
Has already been said, and done.
Is life progressing, or degenerating?
Just look around and see.
Technology may be innovative,
But it's Babel as plain as can be.
People like to *babble on*,
And bring in a one world order.
Nimrod thought the same thing, too,
But God cut down his border.
How long will man be blind to God,
And live unto himself?
What shall it profit to gain the world,
And end up an erratic elf?
There once was a flood; and fire and brimstone
Rained upon the earth.
From the beginning of time man tempts the Lord,
And evil likes to birth
Error into the minds and hearts
Of men, but if they could
Turn around, and taste and see;
They'd see the Lord is good.
God makes the sun shine on the just,
And on the unjust, too.
He makes the rain to fall upon
The ground for both to view.
He raises crops, and feeds the cows,
And sheep, and goats, and donkeys.
He gives man dwelling from the cold,
And protection from the monkeys.
Darwin may have looked around

In all civility...
To see that man was still evolving,
But never was set free.
Darwin leaned on his own understanding,
And the wisest man said, "No!"
God says what is the absolute truth,
And an arguer's His foe.
If man wants wisdom from the world,
The world will pass away.
If man wants wisdom from on High;
He first must be abased.
There's only one thing that is true;
It's God's way, or it's not.
Anything else is fallacy
That's a devilish, lying plot.
So, man's the monkey in the middle
If Darwin wants some praise,
But praise belongs to God alone
'Cause only He can raise
Man from the dead; though trickery runs
Deep as fiery pits,
And snakes bite hard, and dragons fly,
And scorpion stings can hit
The places that cause drolly pain
With taunting voices o'er,
And shrieky cries of hopelessness
As the raven cries, "Never more,"
But life on earth is bittersweet,
And the strong in God survive
Until God says it's time to go---
It's best to be among the wise.

So Long America

History keeps repeating itself,
And no one wants to listen.
God can choose another nation
To shine, and pay attention.
God is not an American,
He's a God of the Jewish nation,
And Jews are scattered all over the globe---
God is in frustration.
People play God, and think it's right,
But Pharisees are wrong.
A little bit of leaven leaveneth the lump,
And America can be gone.
America lives under captivity
And can go further, and further along;
Until she repents, captivity will stay;
And where will be her song?
Woe unto you who call evil good,
And good evil in those days...
Self-righteous do-gooders make God mad,
For that is not His way.
Repent, and turn while we still can,
Or we will pass away.
Can God so choose another "light"
Besides the U.S.A?
America's label isn't good,
And people continue to provoke
God Almighty with their lack of knowledge,
And their uneven yoke.
She's out of "sync" with God, and mock;
Thinking He's a joke.
It's obvious that America's blind;
Can't people see we're broke?
America's starving, but people think fat's

Better than baby's candy
It's poisoned food, and parasites
That make the fat so dandy.
Health in America's at a low,
And people love their brandy...
So, they ignore the situation,
Or follow after Ghandi.

America, Oh, America

Presidents come, and Presidents go,
And do we have a better country?
We're barbaric, insensitive people who show
That money's the god called "Prosperity."
How can a president be God Almighty?
He's only a mortal creation,
And the separation of church and state
Must always be in the equation.
Living in the past inhibits progression;
It's there as a constant reminder
Of what is good, and what is bad,
And our future looks bleaker than ever.
In the Word we see that America's gone,
But it's hidden in the Book of Daniel
Which is starting to open to a horrible night
If we don't abide in God's *manual*.
Can anyone turn back the hands of time?
Some can have wishful thinking.
Time ticks on, and doesn't stop,
And a ship can't stop from sinking.
A new America can be a "light."
Jesus comes back before destruction,
And all life on earth is annihilated---
'Cause when God makes a promise, it's an unction.
Too many philosophize on what is truth,
But they put too much self in the way.
A person can't ever come to reason,
Unless he learns to be abased.
God is someone to be worshipped;
Someone to be honored, and praised.
God is Lord over everything---
Over all man's vain, sinful ways.
God is merciful; long-suffering;

Not willing that any should perish.
He's a two-edged Sword; someone to fear;
But in fearing, we learn to cherish
His greatness, His power; His only Son
That allows man to come to Him---
For without the blood no man can know
The Father, nor His love for him.
A shining light illuminates Truth.
People are commanded to pray.
God puts people in authority,
And the Truth is the only way.
Leaders are sent, and under God
Whether they be bad, or good.
God will punish as He sees fit,
And America needs brotherhood.
From sea to shining garbage dump---
What's man done to our earth?
God'll destroy those who will
Cause it to be a dearth.
Can time stand still as it once did?
All things are possible with God.
Object lessons from the past
Are as rich as a high priest's ephod.
Is escalation stoppable?
Soon can be decades away.
It can be half a century,
And God can do as He may.
The Holy Spirit hovers the earth
Seeking one man God can use---
So God can manifest Himself,
And show His power through.
America hasn't come to completion,
And Dark won't rule the earth;
For Dark's in subjection to the Light,
And Dark lives under a curse.
God looks down upon the earth
To see what man will do.
Will man decide to stand up tall

Like Elisha, and others, too?
Dagon fell, and broke his head.
His arms were broken, too.
Elisha mocked his followers,
And they feared the God of the Jews.
Can America ever become mature?
It lacks much sophistication.
Troubled times lie up ahead,
But God can give restoration.
Who really loves God more than money;
More than idols, or even power---
More than family, country, or even one's self,
And who's the man of the hour?
The President's not the most powerful man.
Nobody knows who is...
Jesus comes back when we think not,
But escalation still exists.
America hasn't suffered yet---
Enough to know to repent,
And one day she'll fall down to her knees,
And God will straighten what's bent.

Jerusalem, Oh Jerusalem

The Hebrews were cursed to wander around---
For rebelling against the Lord.
They're eyes are darken, and hearts are blacken...
A curse made them divorced.
They wail now at an empty wall---
Thinking God will hear their cries.
God heard Abel's blood cry out...
From the ground when he had died.
No one can fill a prophecy---
Apart from the working of God.
Man must be in synchronization...
With what's written in His Word.
People pray for Jerusalem's peace---
They call it a holy land...
Where people kill, and never cease.
So, where is God in that?
Victories were won in Old Testament times---
But these days war never ceases.
People lean on their own understandings...
And do what they think pleases
Their hearts; but where did they all go---
To selfishness, and to lust?
Peace must come to Jerusalem soon...
Or it may turn to dust.

Win A Way In

The Word of God is a shining Light
Once in the morning, and once at night
David knelt seven times a day
A friend of God is what they say
Absalom hung; cursed on a tree
Solomon strayed, and Jews did flee
Nathan's lineage brought the King
Who rescued man for eternity
But it's by choice, and not by birth
No man can say he'll win by works
An advocate is what man needs
A **Holy High Priest** to intercede
To turn God's wrath away from sin
Or God will surely do one in
He'll toss to hell, and then the abyss
If man won't give the Son a kiss
David knew how to reach God's **Heart**
He looked ahead, as we look back hard
To see with eyes deep in the soul
Not by wordly sights and goals
There is no way, but faith alone
Through grace that leads us safely home
A *Temple* in the Age of Grace
Is all man has to run the race
Through time's deep halls until his grave
And lofty dreams ne'er salvation made
'Tis a gift from God so freely giv'n
To win the race through the doors of Heav'n
And crowns will win if prices are paid
To give to the King; at His feet to lay
To show how much one loves his Lord
And prove his loyal heart's adored
By God who tries the hearts of man

To see who follows His every command
But one can't do it on his own
And that's why God sent His Only Son
Believe and receive one hundred percent
The blood of Jesus; the Innocent
And tell the Father you hate evil ways
Repent, and turn with absolute grace
Open the door, and let Jesus in
To wash away your original sin
With His blood that was shed at Calvary
So, you can be saved, and truly set free

The Enlightenment

In the Age of Enlightenment it is quite clear;
The Darkness of man arose...
To a new level of no return
Through its poetry and prose.

That floats around in the atmosphere;
Out of the devil's domain...
Only the Holy Spirit's thoughts
Bring man a worthwhile gain.

Inside the depths of a person is pride;
An ugly, creeping monster...
Surfacing when the ego's low
Needing a little bolster.

Depression consumes the spirit inside;
For lack of trust in God...
Lust's a growing hideous whelp
Cuddled like peas in a pod.

The pride of life's such a subtle sin;
Many fail to observe...
Fear begins that worthless notion
So many opt to serve.

Be careful for nothing; in everything give thanks;
For this is the will of God...
Trauma damages; few restore
Many have not been taught.

Enlightenment needs to come to the Church;
It's virtue that people lack...
Everyone only cares for their own
Who's there to pick up the slack?

God will fill in, but He uses His people;
Body parts are scattered awry...
Eyes can't see, and ears can't hear
So, Jesus can't come for His Bride.

If earth has the only intelligent form;
Of life in outer space...
I shudder to think of what is beyond
When out of my shell I race.

To unknown realms of the created worlds;
Not known to mortals here...
God will carry me through, I know
Perhaps to a galaxy of ears.

Ears that are made to listen to God;
And harmonious symphonies...
Reverberating in circular motion
In space amid galaxies.

Or ears with eyes to see all the sights;
Of colors intermixed...
And mouths to sing praise to God
With hearts on Him that're fixed.

In the Age of Enlightenment few could grasp;
The true atmospheric Light...
Causing reform helping man know
To live by faith; not sight.

It is easier to live by what man can see;
Than believe the truth of Life...
Pride must go, and lust must flee
And man must conquer strife.

Love must reign, but it only can come;
If love's giv'n the Creator...
God gives it back to love oneself
Then he can love his neighbor.

Will man ever mature to a higher love;
And do away with leaven...
So, God's Kingdom will come; His will be done
On earth as it is in Heav'n?

Enlightenment came, and man crucified;
The Heart that tried to show...
Where the *True Light* really is
But man wants Dark to grow.

The Paradox of Life

The bottom line is self-preservation;
Man cares only for himself---
What keeps him alive, and makes him function
Is to seek happiness, and wealth.

Giving little thought about a future life
Is furthest from his mind---
What's happening in the here, and now
Causes him to be blind.

Parody of life is funny because
The here, and now is eternal---
It's only a consciousness---a state of mind,
But his thoughts remain on the carnal.

What is success, but an illusioned dream,
And everyone's in their own world---
It's hard to learn to step *out of the box*
So, he remains like a snail that's curled

In his own little shell, and only comes out
If it benefits his appetites---
There are a few who truly know and seek
The hidden secrets of life.

Energy and matter once into existence
Cannot ever dissipate---
So, they go into one place or another,
But who can know the date

That the soul will leave when the body's gone?
It better be disconnected---
Because if it's not at the point of death
No life will be resurrected.

Man is deluded to think he's animal,
But that delusion is a plan of God---
For there's an order in this universe,
And a saga that has a plot.

The story of man was written before
The foundation of this second earth---
The first was without form, and void,
And few know the true "rebirth."

That term is used in so many ways,
Because man imagines the vain---
Those who really seek the Truth---
Will be satisfied, and unlike *Cain*.

We are either *Able*, or we're not
To understand the Truth---
Wide is the road that leads to destruction;
Life's path is known to a few.

Many are called, but few are chosen,
Which doesn't include all man---
But the paradox still remains the same;
It's all just part of the plan.

The Starfish

We are what we are, and will be what we'll be...
Our experiences in life push us to our destiny---
We can't change a thing; it's already planned out;
We come in on cue; play our part, and bow out,

But the part that we play makes us a villain or star...
And no one can alter their designated part---
The story was written, and Heav'n sees the play;
They "cheer," or they "boo," to whatever they may.

The Author is crowned with laurels of praise...
And applause rings for all His literary displays---
Watching man flounder, or swim like a whale
Is up to the person who lives in the tale.

Dreaded are souls who swim in the abyss...
Purging forever, giving Jesus a "kiss"---
Thirty pieces of silver shined in their eyes
And they soon ran away to go swim in the lies.

Willy was free, and made his escape...
Billy was humble, and swam to the cape---
Jiminy was jumping, and got caught by a lure;
Bowie was knifed when the rod pulled him sore.

Fishers of men catch many in a net...
And what a reward those fishers will get---
They'll shine like the stars in their part of the play
And Heav'n will applaud their laurels someday.

The waters are filled with various channels...
That run into tributaries, rivers, and canals---
The oceans are deep, and frightening to some
But few have the faith to take the great plunge,

And some find small crevices to cower, and hide...
While some have the desire to swim with the tide---
Some go in waters at such a great risk
And fly like the birds; and plunge into mists.

The paradox lies in swimming in schools...
There's no fish that obeys all of the rules---
Each one's unique, and important to God;
To His purpose, His glory; His story that's odd,

Because odd as it is, God watches and waits...
To see what's inside at each different phase---
And tests every creature that He gives a free will
To see if that one can fill the bill.

The ones who are blotted out of "The Book"...
Will one day find out about the fish's hook---
And the fisherman's rod is not a comforting net
But a jawbreaking shock right into the neck.

Believe, and receive deep into the soul...
God's unspeakable gift, so one can be whole---
And swim in the lakes in space above time
Where life is eternal, and the waters sublime.

Consider The Ant

There were two cities that used to be;
Sodom and Gomorrah,
But now they're gone, and just bywords...
As written in the Torah.

Man can't reason with brains as peas;
Like ants have brains as salt,
But ants can be admired more...
Because they have no fault.

Consider the ant, and all his ways,
And you will find a truth...
How man is meant to live on earth,
And how he wastes his youth.

We are from dirt; from miry clay,
And not amoeba and apes;
For their beginnings appeared before...
Man was ever made.

Become a brick and you'll be crushed;
It's better to be clay...
To be molded into something grand,
And not degenerate.

Pollute the good and bad will remain;
'Til stars fall from the sky...
Corrupt all nature and the perfect order
If you really want to cry.

There is no limit to greed of gain;
For it's a bottomless pit,
And one day there'll be a reckoning...
Into faces that God will spit.

God is holy; someone to be feared,
And all the ungodly will wail.
There'll be no relief for the damages done...
That have left an empty trail.

No religion knows everything;
They all have a slant on the Truth.
Maybe a few see the picture head-on...
Waiting to come into view.

God chooses whom He wills to bless,
And destroys as He so pleases;
So, it's better to be on the winning side...
Before the temporal life ceases.

Count Me In

Zero stands for eternity, and one symbolizes God...
Two, God talks poignantly... repetition is a rod.

Two can mean unity; for two can fellowship;
Three is Godhead; not Trinity; triangles corner and trip.

Four to me is mercy given; five is grace alone...
Six is a number of a man; seven is completion.

Eight is a new beginning; circles go on forever;
New beginnings in God will reap His perfect favor.

Nine is a number of God along with new beginnin'
Ten is God, and eternity; the others are repetition.

There is no demonic number; Dewey had a system;
The devil only copies, and God has him in derision.
God uses many numbers, and also symbolism...
Rule life by mathematics; it's numerology forbidden.

People worship creation, and all God's attributes;
Don't worship His Spirit; He deserves the tribute.

He lifts His Son to glorify; to magnify His name...
Jesus' name is powerful; His blood is also the same.

Jesus seeks the Father's will; bows to His Excellency;
The Father lifts up His Son; to crown His Majesty.

Saints lift others higher than self; so, it is written...
That's how God operates; eternal lovin', and givin'.

Give more than one takes, and always seek to give;
Put others over self, and so, it's in Christ we live.

Jesus died with ultimate love; no greater love is this...
That a man lays down his life; to save all of His friends.

Count me in for I want all God wants to freely give;
Count me in for I want all His love eternally in Him.

Love's eternal with no end; neither is God's mercy...
Souls who won't come to God will be amid the cursed.

Always count your blessings, and thank God for *HE IS*;
Be counted worthy to escape the everlasting abyss.

He wants man's full dependency; nothing else will do
Until man fully understands, the trials seem so huge.

As the years progress each day; self will be no more;
Count me in 'cause I want God to live inside my core.

Don't Be Afraid

Little school girl, little school girl---run on home;
The wolves are all howling, so don't be afraid.

Little school boy, little school boy---run on home...
The coyotes are all growling, so don't be afraid.

Little mommy, little mommy---run to God and sing;
The men are all snarling, so don't be afraid.

Little daddy, little daddy---run under Abba's wing...
The women aren't all darling, so don't be afraid.

Li'l soldier, li'l soldier---pound hard on your drum;
The enemy's at your front door, so don't be afraid.

Li'l bachelor, li'l bachelorette---don't be so numb;
God is your helper, so don't be afraid.

Little toddler, little toddler---run to your crib...
The T.V.'s biting hard, so don't be afraid.

Little baby, little baby---in your little bib;
God has you in His arms, so don't be afraid.

Little old one, little old one---shine like a star...
Pray on your knees, so don't be afraid.

Little cripple, little cripple---stay where you are;
Angels are watching thee, so don't be afraid.

The Kingdom

Military might's what people think is right...
God will cause wars to cease---
He scattered the people who delighted in war,
And broke them into pieces.
God is peace, and God is Love...
All nations shall praise the Lord---
For He is God; His name is "Jah,"
And God always honors His Word.
He sets the solitary in families...
And He reigns to judge the poor---
The fatherless; the widows He'll recompense,
And wealth He'll lay up in store.
Fear the Lord, and depart from evil...
Cleave to that which is good---
There is no help in man, it's written,
And God will bring brotherhood.
Man must repent, and get out of the way...
For God to show how terrible---
He is among the peoples on earth,
And that He is so reliable.
He saves the ones who want salvation...
And destroys the wicked with fire---
A sword shall pierce into their bellies,
And He will show His power.
God is someone to be feared...
For He is the Almighty Maker---
His sword is a sharp, double, two-edged sword,
He is the Omniscient Protector.
God loves the sinner, but hates the sin...
And sent His only Son---
To save the world from eternal damnation,
And wants all nations to come
Into His Kingdom which is spiritual...

It's not a place on earth---
The only way to get inside
Is to have the proper rebirth.
So many people imagine vain things...
But there is only one way---
Repent to the only One True God;
Jehovah is His name.
Ask Jesus, His Son to wash away sin...
That man was born into---
And come inside to dwell forever;
To reign in a Temple not hewn
In stone, nor steel, nor golden columns...
For symbols are what God uses---
Only through eyes God opens up
Can man ever learn to love Jesus.
Let His Kingdom come; on earth be done...
Let all nations praise the Lord---
For He is holy, and man is lost;
Let's praise Him in one accord.
And love Him for His unspeakable gift...
The perfect sacrifice---
For God so died to set man free,
And give him paradise.
His Kingdom isn't in this world...
It's spiritual beyond all measure---
His family will live in happiness, and peace,
And bask in all His treasures.

Trivial Living

The "Greats" have come and they have gone---
Made remarks in history...
Van Gogh said this earth is a "mere sketch,"
But God has certainty.
We're coming to the end of time---
As plain as days drag on...
No one will change a thing because
The Author's Spirit will be gone.
In what is written in volumes of man---
On this second planet earth...
One must know it's time to go
To the Arch---the door of rebirth.
Prayer can change a situation---
In the Age of Grace...
But when God's wrath hits this planet earth,
Things are a different case.
The Age of Grace is a phenomenon---
Where impossible things can be done...
It's an Age of endless time before
Prophecy that's told will come.
Man wastes time like youth wastes life---
When so much progress can be...
An escalation of nothing but progression
Into heights of eternity.
But man travels in circles in deserts so much---
He can't see what lies ahead...
We all face giants in valleys below,
But can man learn to fly instead?

Left Behind

Tit for tat, and mouse turns rat,
And cat and dog run wild---
Birds peck eyes, and mosquitoes fly
To poison the weak and defiled.
Hares bite legs, and toes are curled;
Baldness is all around---
Strong are feeble, and justice will cry
And blood will scream out of the ground.
"Are any spared?" the question lies;
It's hard to say; ask Noah---
Women have wisdom, but venom appears
And gossiping men are boas.
Deadened hearts, and lust runs long,
And people are bored with the former---
Violence breeds violence, and power corrupts
And money's no value to the scorner.
Stars will fall, and mountains will crumble,
And dragons and demons will rise---
Satyrs and unicorns, vultures, and angels
Will appear to the human eyes.
A remnant is all that ever is spared,
Because most just follow the crowd---
That's why man is likened unto sheep
Because to the slaughter they're proud.
Head over heels, and upside down,
The earth will be in amiss---
Evil will reign on top of good
And people will howl and hiss.
Disorder and dread will be one's bread,
And most will have eyes that are blind---
Those who are left to watch and wait
Will know they've been left behind.

Simplicity

Flowers are best when they're left unpicked
So the world can enjoy their beauty;

Courage is only good if one
Can rise to do his duty---

A thankful state is much more fare
Then pleading for a cause;

And gold, and silver are of none effect
If owners killed for their paws---

Tragic times come to all
The minds o'ertaken with bliss;

Music lives in the atmosphere
But discord sets it amiss---

Simplicity is a relative dream
But complex minds do wander;

Idleness is the devil's workshop
And working hands don't ponder---

Beauty is fleeting unless it's inside
Deep in the soul of a few;

And pride's as ugly as viper's scales
That many like to view---

Happiness comes to those who do right
And runs away when chased;

Favor is a blessed state
When it comes from being abased---

Reaching for goals is ignoring the present
One opens up each day;

And a God led life is ecstasy
If one knows how to pray---

Barns and silos full of grain
Cause a soul required;

Loving and giving is by far the best
To ward off the eternal fire---

A fellow man in need of help
Should never be overlooked;

And eating a fish that's raw, and undone
Is worse than being cooked---

Finishing a task is worthy enough
To merit a simple coin;

And he who eats without the labor
Does hurt to his own loin---

Living life without praising God
Is foolish as can be;

For who can add one hair to his head
And set a person free?

Freedom's a choice, but many are bound
And God's the controller of all;

It's best to not turn a deafen ear
And wake up to His call---

We're given gifts to use for God
But hidden treasures are lost;

Teaching to fish, and healing the sick
Is in church that grows no moss---

Ichabod lurks at every corner
And sights on flesh invite

Death to come in, and the Spirit to flee
So tongues of discord bite---

In one accord let's lift holy hands
And praise His Excellency;

For there is none above "*I AM*"
Let all nations fall to their knees---

What statue, or idol can create such beauty
That people can see on earth;

And in the skies, and in the seas
And make animals give birth?

Ask God to take the blinders off
He came to save the lost;

The vilest man who ever lived
Is loved by Almighty God---

Esau He hated, and some have gone
In the way of Cain;

It's man's free will to choose the road
That leads to bliss, or pain---

It's how a person views his life
A matter of the heart;

Will one let God soften that pump
Or, just let it grow hard?

We live in a time where the end is near
Nearer than e'er before;

And time is quickly running out
Don't ignore the "Ark" once more.

Illusions

Life on earth's an illusion; not everything's illusory...
Things have no value; rust and thieves break in;
People placed before us place us to a test---
Things we own are also a trial to surface sin.

The test is clear indeed; do we love God in deeds...
Are things here for lust; or tools to work our faith?
Is man loved by God; through the lights that love;
Is vanity futile...what does the Word saith?

Rush on, Oh flowing rivers; grasp hold of the riviere...
It lasts forever in Heaven; rust and thieves are gone;
This fleeting life is temporal; flee it so you can see---
Don't let the devil trick you; he's known to be a con.

Living in the flesh; makes everything so fleshly...
Grass grows up to fade; new sprouts arise each year;
Life's cycle is forever; earth's circled here before---
A new earth will arise; and few can really hear.

Ears inside the soul; are meant for some to solely...
Reach out among the lost; who can't find their way;
The chosen live on earth to help the others choose;
To salt and light the world; not fly away when saved.

Spend the time in wisdom; winning souls is wise...
Living life in pleasure; gets burned up in the fire;
Enjoy the fruits of labor; Day is time to work---
Night soon comes before us; be lifted from the mire.

Contentment

Market yourself, and you'll be the loser---
Pocket yourself, and you'll be the chooser;
Laugh at yourself, and you'll be a winner...
Despise yourself, and be a big sinner.
Pray to yourself, and you'll get no answer---
Worship yourself, and you're a tiny dancer;
Look at yourself, and forget what you're after...
Run from yourself and you'll feel the laughter.

Study yourself, and you'll understand more---
Pride yourself, and you'll be a bore;
Simplify yourself, and life will be sweeter...
Curse yourself, and you'll be a cheater.
Balance yourself, and you may live longer---
Punish yourself, and you won't be any stronger;
Accept yourself, and all of your failings...
Strengthen yourself, and do all your wailings,
Because after that...is contentment.

When I Think About

When I think about people, it leaves a hole in my heart
When I think about Jesus, He fills up that part---
When I think about money, it leaves me empty;
When I think about eternity, I think of plenty.

When I think about nature, it's pretty to see
When I think about animals, they really scare me---
When I think about oceans, they cause separation;
When I think about lakes, they're beautiful creations.

When I think about cities, they confuse and congest
When I think of the country, I think about rest---
When I think about seagulls, I think about hawks;
When I think about cardinals, I think they talk.

When I think about bushes, I think about blockades
When I think about flowers, I think about bouquets---
When I think of snow falling, I think about chills;
When I think about doctors, I think about pills.

When I think about food, I think about necessity
When I think about sleep, I yearn for that destiny---
When I think about escape, I think of God's grace;
When I think about His Word, I think about praise.

When I think about reason, I think about faith
When I think about science, I think about space---
When I think about flying, I think about clouds;
When I think about trumpets, I think what's loud.

When I think about Heaven, I think about time
When I think about the aged, I think about a climb---
When I think about ladders, I think of Jacob's dream;
When I think about chariots, I think a fiery limousine.

Prayer In The Garden

Everyone thinks I'm just "in a mood"...
They think I'll snap back, and come out of it.
They don't even realize whom I really am,
And never dreamed I grew away from their pit.

Time will go by, and all they will have...
Is a memory with a loss, that they'll regret.
I'm only a human, and I'm not immortal,
Save my inner man who chooses to forget.

Pains, and afflictions others caused in my life...
Knowingly or unknowingly; I surely can bet
Their loss will be great; they can't take it back,
Because I'm just not God to forgive and forget.

I'm human enough to forgive through my Lord...
But to be alone in solitude is what my mind's set.
With Jesus I'm filled; I am all alone;
We're only but mortal, and I'm owed a great debt;

They can't e'er repay, so I forgive them all...
All that I want are my memories I've kept.
I find great fulfillment in things not of earth;
Not people, nor animals, nor anything adept.

People are all basically the same...
Have I done the same to others? I'm sure;
But some are takers, and seldom ever give,
And that's why I don't see them anymore.

Simplicity of life in my own little world...
Is happiness to me once everything is swept,
And all that remains is my Saviour, and Lord;
I remember the passage that says, "Jesus wept."

An Artist's Verse

A starving artist is known as such; he seeks above the rest
Of mediocre, mechanical machines; busy li'l bees progress
Serving a Queen to pamper her; she doesn't a thing at all;
 Lays down laws, taxes and terms; drones hear her call.

A kingly man who follows God is humble, fair, and just...
He's indeed a rare commodity; absolute power corrupts;
People desire figureheads; denying to think on their own,
Cause God seems delusive; hard to find; hard to be known.

Is laziness in man stopping him from knowing God at all?
Adam knew; woman...deceived; she caused man to fall;
 Every offspring from then on; comes from fallen man...
Sin bears him; redemption saves him; that's the only plan.

Can man play God; redeem himself; if he's not worthy to?
Peacocks are proud; ostriches scared; what is man to do?
Answers are given by God everyday; who cares to listen?
Humility and diligence pave the way; bringing in reason.

Methodical rituals; vanity and verse; monotony and chills
Deceptive vain traditions of man; the devil tricks with skill
 Carnal love is earthly and devilish; it distorts the mind;
 God's love serves; doesn't take...except mud off the blind.

The top of everything is God; He died, and then arose...
So man can have true love at last; see past his own nose;
Artists strive to paint a scene; in genres for many minds;
They want others to know the hurts; buried deep inside.

The hurts are there from experience; they teach realities
One can't learn from reading texts; artists serve the bees.
 Being bees are easier; they buzz all around the honey...
Solitary, starving artists live to please without the money.

Wisdom Speaks

Passing the time isn't sublime
Unless there's reason, and rhyme.
Doing a feat can be ever so sweet
To occupy an idle mind.
Living a life in vanity, and strife
Brings aging to the young.
Gambling away one's hard earned pay
Is nothing other than dumb.
A wise man holds, and doesn't scold,
But waits for calamity...
After warning is done, and all of the fun
Has reached its ultimate peak.
Giving to needy, and not being greedy
Out of one's abundance is well;
Hoarding one's riches leaves one in ditches
Driving many others to hell.
Vanity of life is many a man's wife
That he loves more than anything.
He thinks Heav'n can wait, but it'll be too late,
And time will fly faster than wings.
Abasing one's self to his Maker is wealth,
And someday will rise to the heights,
If he holds on by faith; not tossed by a wave,
And he learns to fight the good fight.
Reaching for dreams are illusive it seems
'Cause dreams come to those who wait.
Simplicity is light, and makes one's plight
So very uncomplicated.
Virtue is better than to owe a debtor;
Climbing out of a hole,
And thinking of flesh is only a test
To see what's inside the soul.

March On Young Men

Warriors know step, and song...
Who's to say that we'll live long?
Good is on our side if greed
Doesn't take the reins to lead.
One, two...one, two; shake the legs, and be on cue...
Three, four...three, four; do a li'l dance and give it more

Marching is the energy...
Brotherhood's our euphony.
We will fight for what is right;
The battle's won; God's on our side.
One, two...one, two; shake the legs, and be on cue...
Three, four...three, four; do a li'l dance and give it more

Power comes in unity...
We will fight to set men free.
Hold our arms, and heads up high
We will march 'til we can fly.
One, two...one, two; shake the legs, and be on cue...
Three, four...three, four; do a li'l dance and give it more

Notorious we'll come on home
God is our protective dome...
He will fight for us always
He will give us length of days...
One, two...one, two; shake the legs, and be on cue...
Three, four...three, four; do a li'l dance and give it more

Trimming The Fat

God is a judge of the thoughts and intents
In every person's life.
He knows who abases himself to Him,
And who lifts himself on high.

God resists all man's foolish pride,
But giveth grace to the humble.
He notices everything far and wide,
And He sees when people stumble.

Judgment comes before Judgment Day
To all that strain at a gnat.
We reap what's sewn in seasons someday,
And meat's trimmed from the fat.

Fat will burn, and meat will char,
But a perfect prime of cut
Is a savory choice of a delicate art
That melts on the Almighty's tongue.

Tie A Yellow Ribbon

Tie a yellow ribbon around a package,
And put something cherished inside.
It doesn't need to be costly nor new;
It only needs to arrive
'To the hands of one you think's not worthy;
To someone you don't like...
Give it with love, and not of yourself,
And you'll see that person cry.
Love is shining all around you,
And everywhere you go---
His name's not Eros, Cupid, nor Erotes;
He's Agape set into Phileo.
Her name is Charity who's love in action;
Not a feeling that comes and goes---
That person's usually in front of you;
Standing under your nose.
Tie a ribbon around your finger,
To remind you to think of another.
Make it yellow symbolizing friendship;
And you might gain a brother.
It's always nice to have a new sister,
And also another mother...
God's family lacks many family members,
'Cause the carnal likes to smother.
To have a working family,
That in God they do abide---
Is God's most earnest desire to see;
So Jesus can come for His Bride.
Nonfunctional, disjointed, dispersed and down
It needs to be on fire;
Return to Your first Love, and the first works;
The Church seems to have crossed wires.

Make Way, Make Way!

Make way, make way, the King will come...
Roll out the red carpet, and put away fun---

Go against your grain, and make yourself ready;
For the King is coming; no time to be petty.

Put on white robes that are washed in the blood...
Put on His holiness, live in purity and love---

Repent of your evils; have your oil lamp burning;
Turn from sinfulness; and have a deep yearning

To bow at His presence the moment He arrives...
Make way, make way; He's coming by surprise---

Pray that you be worthy to be His chosen Bride;
Don't assume anything, or you're following a lie.

The hour soon cometh, and no one will know
When the King will arrive to take His eloped.

He'll come back again, a second time through...
Maybe you'll make it before you are doomed

To have your head fly away from your body,
And His second coming will be seen by everybody.

Every knee shall bow, and every tongue confess
That Jesus is Lord; He's the King at His best.

Philosophie de Caul

Where will you go when you will die?
Will you go to hell, or Heaven?
How do you know, or do you just surmise?
Life without knowing isn't reason.

Existing is life that many just do,
And pleasure is all they know.
When pleasure ceases to come into view,
What will one have to show?

The older a person grows he's proud,
And can't figure out truth in life.
Life's merely habitual; one follows the crowd,
And the majority travels the wide.

Narrow's the way that few can find;
The road to eternal salvation---
Why is that true many lag behind
When God is the Author of Creation?

God makes the rules that people must follow,
'Cause if left to one's self to know---
One can philosophize 'til exhaustion runs hollow,
And may look in the eyes of a crow.

Caskets are closed from so many fearing,
And those who are close to dying
See demons coming or angels appearing;
At which time there'll be no more vying.

No one by reason can merit goodness.
Paradise is where man's prone to sin.
Adversity brings man into repentance,
And punishment comes to all men---

For none are good; no, not one,
Or Jesus just died in vain.
All is vanity under the sun,
But under the Son goodness reigns.

Man can't achieve that on his own;
If he could, the cross was a waste,
And nothing God does is vanity; or known
Unless His Spirit illuminates.

Will man give his life as a sacrifice,
And deny himself, and desires
To please his Creator, and give up vice,
And pass through Shadrach's fire?

Unless man has a perfect walk
With God through His only Son,
Then, the Holy Spirit will truth unlock
To reveal His Word to some.

With God alone through thick and thin,
And through all adversity;
How much is man willing to spend
For the price to be set free?

Everything happens according to plan,
But the paradox of life's complex.
It's choices that determine outcomes and
Changes things that can vex---

Through prayers and supplications made;
Through hearts of gold offerings
God takes note, and one must wait
For time, and love, and things.

God's Kingdom can come to life on this earth
To all who desire salvation---
For all man is offered God's blessed rebirth,
And all can be a new creation;

But selfishness never renders rewards,
And many are insensitive
To the sufferings that others must endure,
But those are not God's intents.

God wants man's love first of all,
And love others as himself---
To restore the breach made by the fall,
And care about Heaven's wealth.

The only way to the Father is this:
Repentance to a Holy Creator,
And ask His Son to wash away sin,
With His blood, and dwell inside forever;

To believe completely without any falter
That Jesus will make His abode---
To wash away sin---past, present, and future,
And come into dwell in one's soul.

God has a perfect order of things;
It's not nature that man's to love,
But it's only God in eternity
So, man must give everything up.

Happiness comes, and happiness goes,
As sadness does the same;
Opposites show us pleasure, and woe,
So, man can have a gain.

If people are born in deformities;
God is a mighty healer.
He lets things happen to show His power,
But faith is the mighty sealer.

If some die young, it's for man to see
That the living are strong, and endure---
It's mercy, or punishment among other things,
And only God can know for sure.

Is it possible for earth to be complete;
God's Kingdom come as in Heaven?
If man can ever win over defeat,
And free himself from leaven---

With God all things are possible,
And earth can be as it should---
The way God intended is plausible;
Where evil flies from good;

Where good abounds in every soul---
In purity and holiness;
That comes when one is finally whole,
Not through man's made-up gist.

Will suffering ever cease to birth?
One day when all is well---
Will that ever happen here on earth?
It's only God who can tell,

But God leaves man to make his bed,
And learn to sleep in it;
To teach him not to bump his head,
And lay in springs, and pits,

And when man learns to overcome,
He'll then show others how
To lovingly learn to walk; then run,
And sleep in peaceful clouds.

In asking God if it's lonely at the top,
He said, "No," (He has His Son;
They feed off each other, and never stop,
And live in blissful fun).

God created man to love Him
As the angels in Heaven do.
What has God created so vast
In royal colors, and hues?

What glorious symphonies and stars
To sparkle and shine like jewels
From tiny, inerrant mixtures by far,
And from atoms, and molecules---

To put man in such awe, and wonder
Forever in eternity---
Eye hath not seen, nor ear ever heard
What God has in His store of beauty!

The Son came out of the bosom of God,
For the purpose of saving man.
He came down from Heaven to be a rod
To guide, and to die as the Lamb.

We feed off of Jesus who is the Word.
He's the Bread of Life, and more;
He's the Living Water so man won't thirst.
He's an "arch"---an open door.

We drink His blood, and eat His body
To feed off Him forever.
It's all symbolism, paradox, and irony,
It's realism, and mystery, but never

Impure, nor are they man-made thoughts;
For the ways of God are holy;
But God uses human terms a lot,
So, man can decipher His glory.

To unbelievers it's nonsense, and pallid
For pride just stands in the way---
But to understand the mysteries of God
One first must learn to be abased.

So, the philosophies man's ever dreamt
Have always been based on pride.
Man wants to follow the devil's tempt
'Stead of reflecting what's inside.

In God's knowledge, understanding and wisdom
With humility by grace through faith;
Man can receive an absolute pardon,
And be led down that narrow way.

Through pompous ways, and self-indulgence,
And living in vanity---
A short-lived living life to death
Is seen by Kings and Queens.

No matter what one status he bears
All are not created equal.
The reason being is so others can share
With hurting, and needy people.

We share our things, our love, our time,
Our faith, ourselves, our prayers---
To make another's crooked line
A road that they can bear.

It's God who knows the real truth,
And where true happiness lies.
Man merely tries to be a sleuth;
To end up in compromise.

Religion's a man-made organization,
But Jesus is not a religion.
He's befitting for every single occasion,
And He's not a living legend.

He's God Almighty in the form of flesh;
He died for the sins of man;
And all who come to Him for rest
Will have Heaven in the palm of their hand.

Epilogue

How can one know of God if it wasn't through His Word alone? Jesus *IS* the Word of God made flesh. See John 1:1, and I John 5:7. Just as there are a lot of names for God, there are also a lot of names for His Heart. One can see that God is very diversified and complex if there are nine attributes to His Holy Spirit and there are seven Spirits of God found in the Hebrew Scrolls. The Word has no end, because God has no end. Man is limited. Unless something is Holy Spirit inspired and led, it is not able to be trusted. One must trust one hundred percent in something of God first before God will reveal the Truth.

"Look unto me, and be ye saved, all the ends of the earth: for I *am* God, and there is none else." (Isaiah 45:22)

Printed in the United States
By Bookmasters